THE DEADLY RACE
TO THE SOUTH POLE

by John Micklos, Jr. • illustrated by Paul McCaffrey

CAPSTONE PRESS
a capstone imprint

Graphic Library is published by Capstone Press, an imprint of Capstone.
1710 Roe Crest Drive
North Mankato, Minnesota 56003
capstonepub.com

Copyright © 2022 by Capstone. All rights reserved. No part of this publication may be reproduced in whole or in part, or stored in a retrieval system, or transmitted in any form or by any means, electronic, mechanical, photocopying, recording, or otherwise, without written permission of the publisher.

Library of Congress Cataloging-in-Publication Data
Names: Micklos, John, Jr., author.
Title: The deadly race to the South Pole / by John Micklos, Jr. ; illustrated by Paul McCaffrey.
Description: North Mankato, Minnesota : Capstone Press, 2022. | Series: Deadly expeditions | Includes bibliographical references and index. | Audience: Ages 8-11 | Audience: Grades 4-6 | Summary: "In 1910, Sir Robert Falcon Scott led a team of Englishmen racing to be the first people to reach the South Pole. Amidst frigid temperatures and raging winds, Scott and four others made it to the Pole only to find that another team had gotten there first. Low on morale and facing ever-plunging temperatures, the trek home would prove a harrowing task. Find out if Scott and his men ever made it back home from their frigid adventure"— Provided by publisher.
Identifiers: LCCN 2021029878 (print) | LCCN 2021029879 (ebook) | ISBN 9781663958891 (hardcover) | ISBN 9781666322200 (paperback) | ISBN 9781666322217 (pdf) | ISBN 9781666322231 (kindle edition)
Subjects: LCSH: Scott, Robert Falcon, 1868-1912—Juvenile literature. | Explorers—Great Britain—Biography—Juvenile literature. | Antarctica—Discovery and exploration—British—Juvenile literature. | South Pole—Discoverty and exploration—British—Juvenile literature.
Classification: LCC G875.S35 M53 2022 (print) | LCC G875.S35 (ebook) | DDC 919.8904092/2 [B]—dc23
LC record available at https://lccn.loc.gov/2021029878
LC ebook record available at https://lccn.loc.gov/2021029879

Editorial Credits
Editor: Mandy Robbins; Designer: Dina Her; Media Researcher: Jo Miller; Production Specialist: Tori Abraham

All internet sites appearing in back matter were available and accurate when this book was sent to press.

TABLE OF CONTENTS

On April 6, 1909, explorer Robert Peary became the first-known person to reach Earth's North Pole. The North Pole was one of the last places on Earth to be explored. Peary's feat made front-page news around the world.

Extra, Extra! Read all about it!

Peary reaches the North Pole!

After Peary's success, reaching the South Pole became the next big goal. Teams from Norway and Great Britain raced to get there first. Roald Amundsen led a Norwegian expedition. Captain Robert Falcon Scott led a British team.

On June 15, 1910, the British crew of more than 60 men set sail on the *Terra Nova* from Wales in the United Kingdom. As they did, Captain Scott thought about their upcoming journey.

Australia. New Zealand. Antarctica. The South Pole.

Who knows what adventures and dangers our journey may bring?

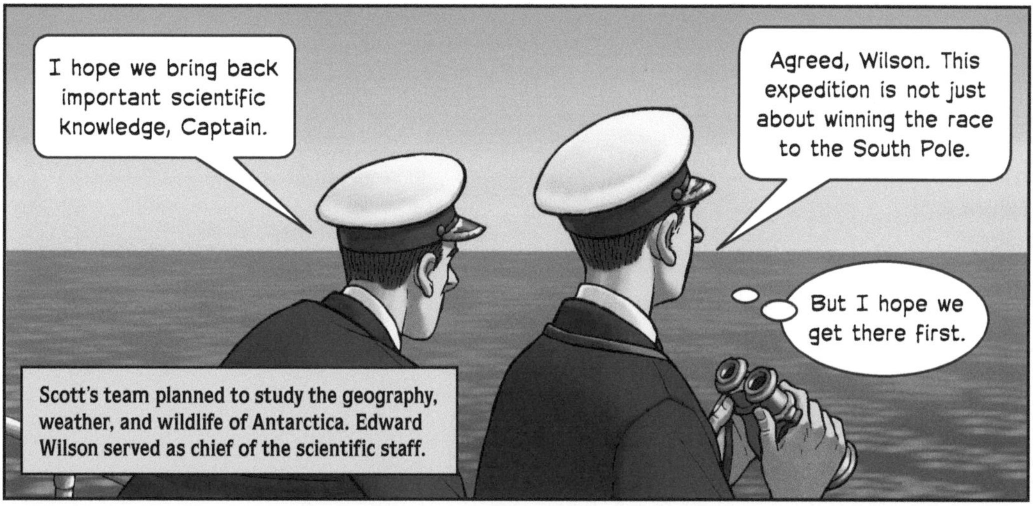
I hope we bring back important scientific knowledge, Captain.
Agreed, Wilson. This expedition is not just about winning the race to the South Pole.
But I hope we get there first.
Scott's team planned to study the geography, weather, and wildlife of Antarctica. Edward Wilson served as chief of the scientific staff.

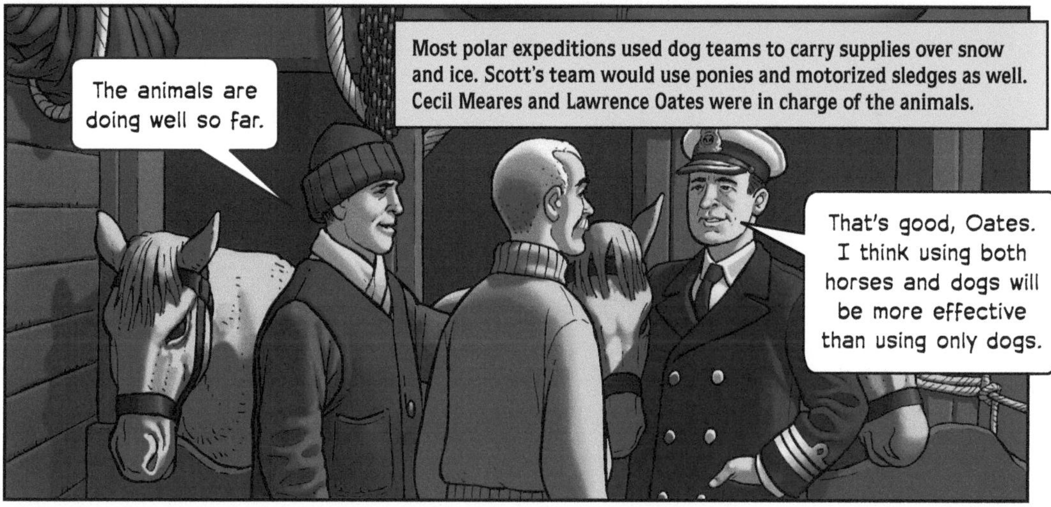
Most polar expeditions used dog teams to carry supplies over snow and ice. Scott's team would use ponies and motorized sledges as well. Cecil Meares and Lawrence Oates were in charge of the animals.
The animals are doing well so far.
That's good, Oates. I think using both horses and dogs will be more effective than using only dogs.

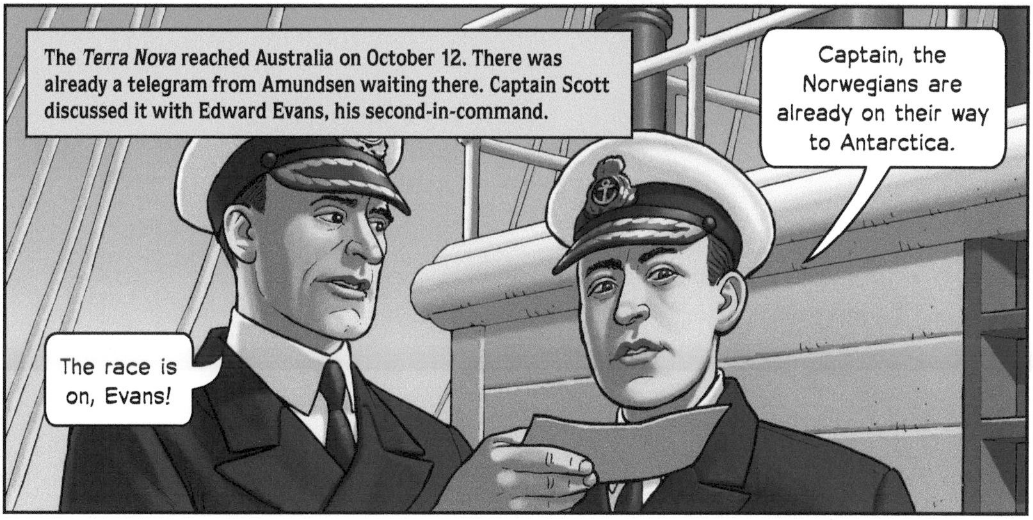
The *Terra Nova* reached Australia on October 12. There was already a telegram from Amundsen waiting there. Captain Scott discussed it with Edward Evans, his second-in-command.
Captain, the Norwegians are already on their way to Antarctica.
The race is on, Evans!

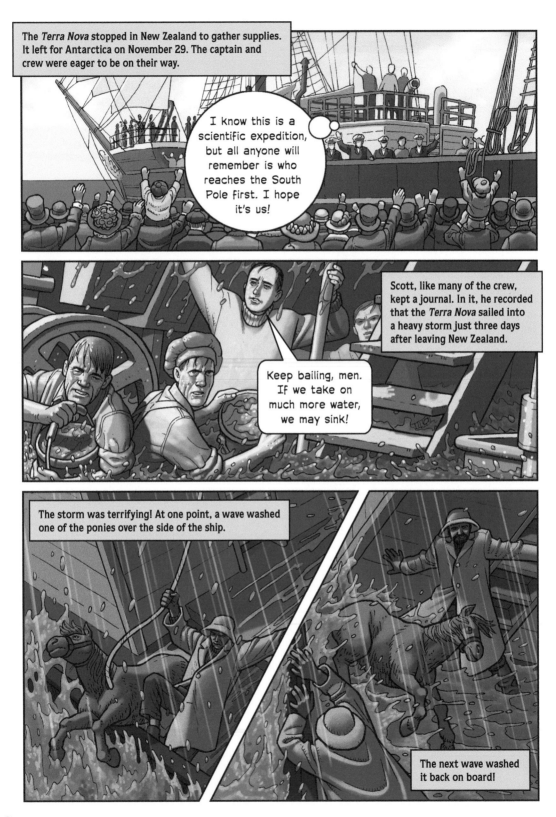

The *Terra Nova* stopped in New Zealand to gather supplies. It left for Antarctica on November 29. The captain and crew were eager to be on their way.

I know this is a scientific expedition, but all anyone will remember is who reaches the South Pole first. I hope it's us!

Scott, like many of the crew, kept a journal. In it, he recorded that the *Terra Nova* sailed into a heavy storm just three days after leaving New Zealand.

Keep bailing, men. If we take on much more water, we may sink!

The storm was terrifying! At one point, a wave washed one of the ponies over the side of the ship.

The next wave washed it back on board!

As the *Terra Nova* drew near Antarctica, a new challenge loomed—icebergs and packed ice! For three weeks the ship could not get near shore. Scott recorded his frustration in his journal.

I can imagine few things more trying to the patience than the long wasted days of waiting.

The crew kept busy. Wilson and assistant zoologist Apsley Cherry-Garrard watched and studied whales, birds, fish, and penguins. Herbert Ponting took photographs.

Finally, the ice broke up. *Terra Nova* sailed toward Antarctica.

The mountains are splendid. I look forward to reaching them.

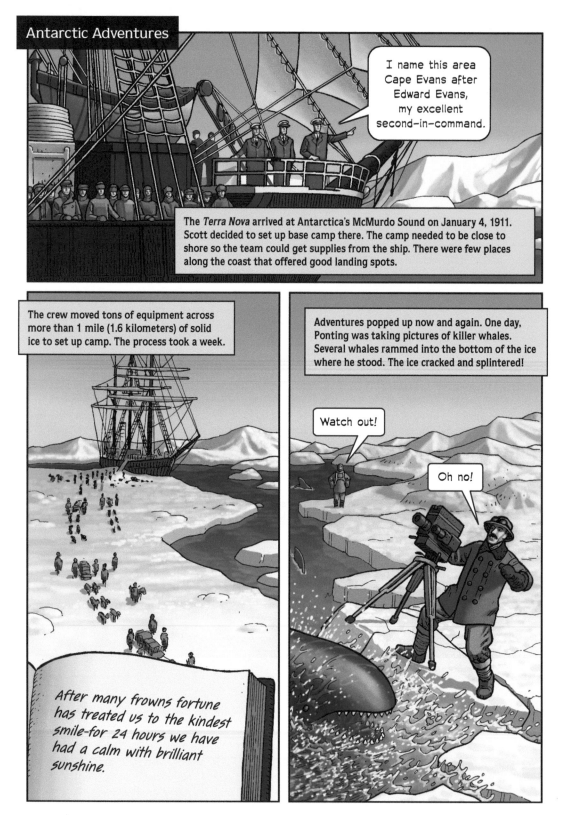

I name this area Cape Evans after Edward Evans, my excellent second-in-command.

The *Terra Nova* arrived at Antarctica's McMurdo Sound on January 4, 1911. Scott decided to set up base camp there. The camp needed to be close to shore so the team could get supplies from the ship. There were few places along the coast that offered good landing spots.

The crew moved tons of equipment across more than 1 mile (1.6 kilometers) of solid ice to set up camp. The process took a week.

After many frowns fortune has treated us to the kindest smile-for 24 hours we have had a calm with brilliant sunshine.

Adventures popped up now and again. One day, Ponting was taking pictures of killer whales. Several whales rammed into the bottom of the ice where he stood. The ice cracked and splintered!

Watch out!

Oh no!

Splintering ice continued to be a problem. On January 8, a sledge broke through the ice. It nearly dragged a crew member under with it.

On January 17, crew members finished building a large hut.

It's freezing outside, but it's warm in here.

It had better be. This will be our home as we prepare for our journey to the Pole.

Meteorologist George Simpson plotted weather patterns. In the meantime, Scott mapped a course to the Pole.

There are only two seasons here—winter and summer.

Winter lasts from March to October. It's way too cold and dangerous to travel then.

Our journey to the Pole and back will take several months. We must wait to start until late October to avoid traveling in winter.

I'll keep tracking weather patterns. The more we know about them, the better our chances for success.

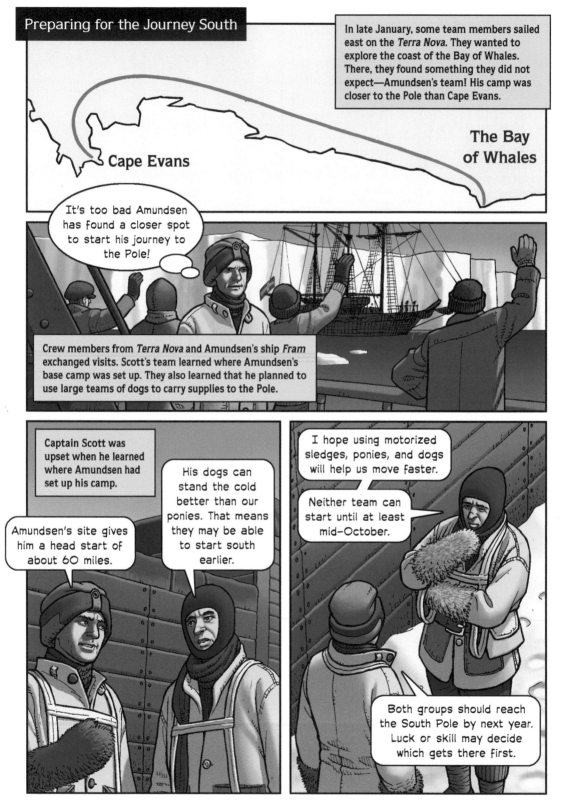

In late January, some team members sailed east on the *Terra Nova*. They wanted to explore the coast of the Bay of Whales. There, they found something they did not expect—Amundsen's team! His camp was closer to the Pole than Cape Evans.

Cape Evans

The Bay of Whales

It's too bad Amundsen has found a closer spot to start his journey to the Pole!

Crew members from *Terra Nova* and Amundsen's ship *Fram* exchanged visits. Scott's team learned where Amundsen's base camp was set up. They also learned that he planned to use large teams of dogs to carry supplies to the Pole.

Captain Scott was upset when he learned where Amundsen had set up his camp.

His dogs can stand the cold better than our ponies. That means they may be able to start south earlier.

Amundsen's site gives him a head start of about 60 miles.

I hope using motorized sledges, ponies, and dogs will help us move faster.

Neither team can start until at least mid-October.

Both groups should reach the South Pole by next year. Luck or skill may decide which gets there first.

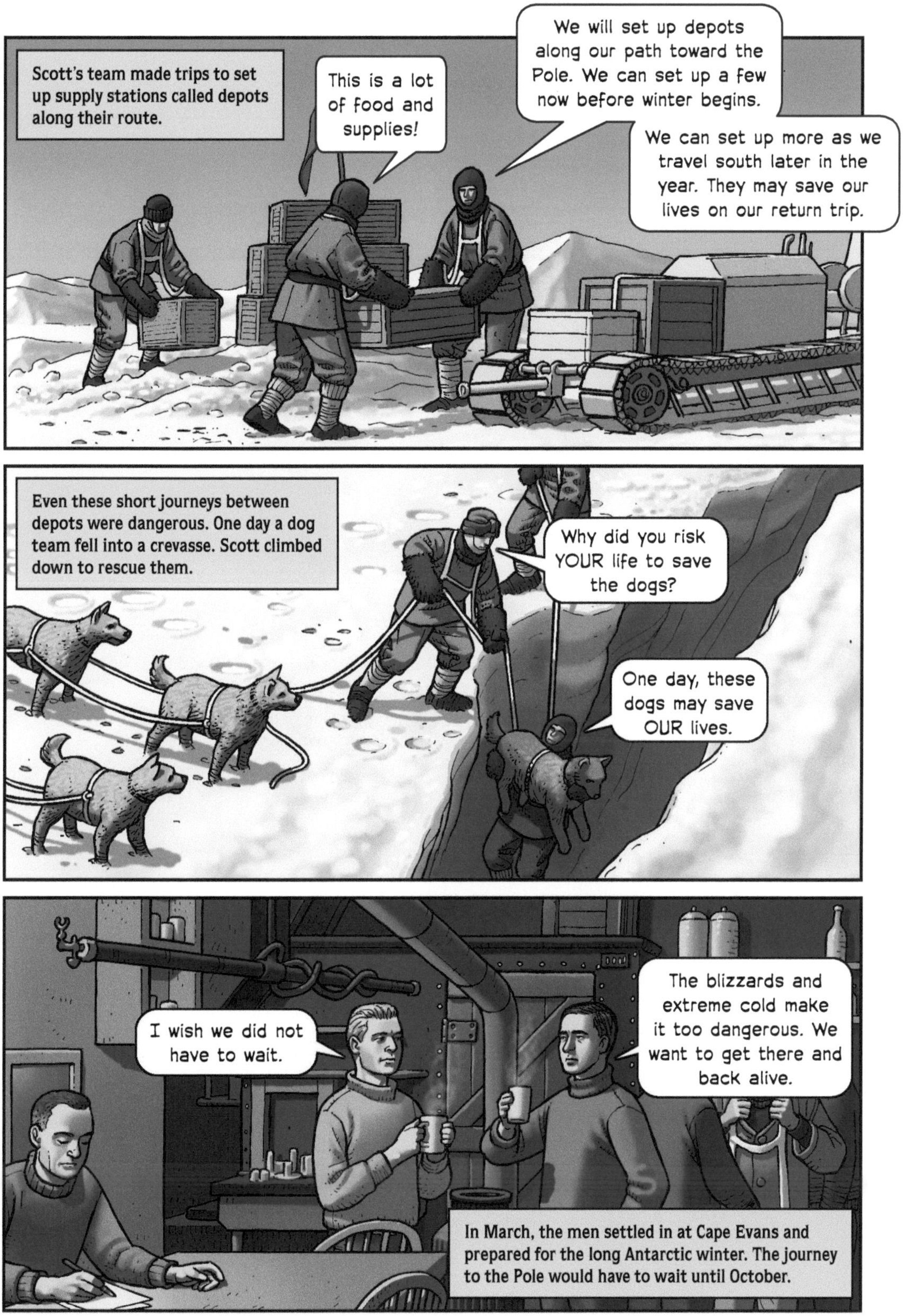
Scott's team made trips to set up supply stations called depots along their route.
This is a lot of food and supplies!
We will set up depots along our path toward the Pole. We can set up a few now before winter begins.
We can set up more as we travel south later in the year. They may save our lives on our return trip.
Even these short journeys between depots were dangerous. One day a dog team fell into a crevasse. Scott climbed down to rescue them.
Why did you risk YOUR life to save the dogs?
One day, these dogs may save OUR lives.
I wish we did not have to wait.
The blizzards and extreme cold make it too dangerous. We want to get there and back alive.
In March, the men settled in at Cape Evans and prepared for the long Antarctic winter. The journey to the Pole would have to wait until October.

Over the winter, crew members at the base camp kept busy. They made short trips to study wildlife and collect rock samples.

Meanwhile, Scott sent teams to set up other camps. One team went west to study valleys and glaciers.

Another team went north to Cape Adare. They studied the area around Mt. Melbourne. This mountain rose nearly 9,000 feet (2,700 meters) high.

In June, Wilson led Cherry-Garrard and Henry Bowers to look for emperor penguin eggs. They hiked 70 miles (113 km). Temperatures dipped below minus 40 degrees Fahrenheit (minus 40 degrees Celsius).

Studying the embryos inside these eggs could reveal if birds and reptiles are related.

The men nearly died on their trek back. A blizzard blew away their tent, so they built a rough igloo of rocks and ice.

I hope we make it back to Cape Evans alive.

We can't die before we even begin our trek to the Pole!

The men finally reached Cape Evans. Other team members had to cut the frozen clothes from their bodies.

You look like a human icicle.

I feel like one.

I hope to never go through anything like that again.

This winter cold can be deadly. We must wait for milder weather before we head south.

Little did Bowers know that worse dangers were yet to come.

Journey to the Pole

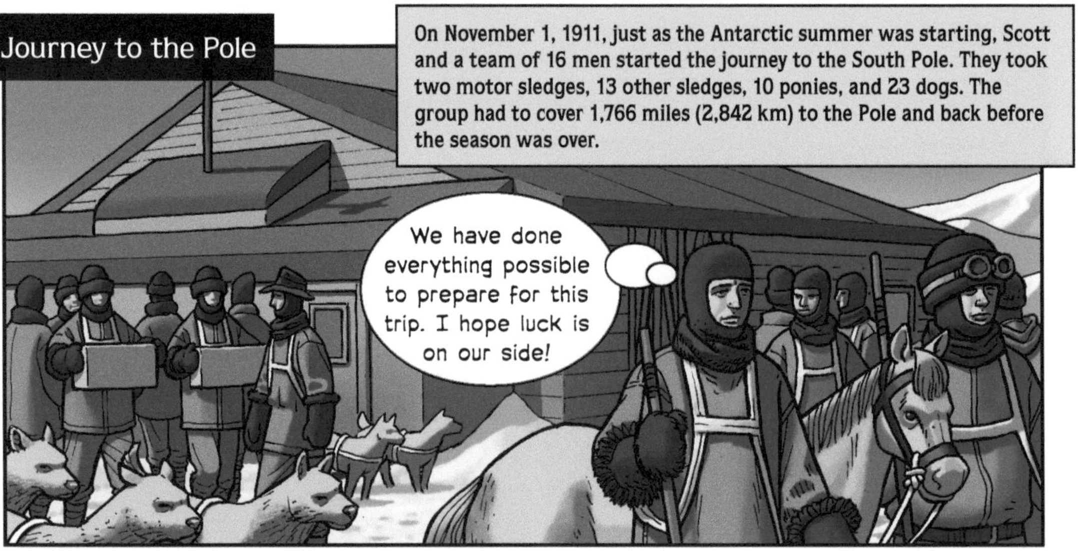
On November 1, 1911, just as the Antarctic summer was starting, Scott and a team of 16 men started the journey to the South Pole. They took two motor sledges, 13 other sledges, 10 ponies, and 23 dogs. The group had to cover 1,766 miles (2,842 km) to the Pole and back before the season was over.
We have done everything possible to prepare for this trip. I hope luck is on our side!

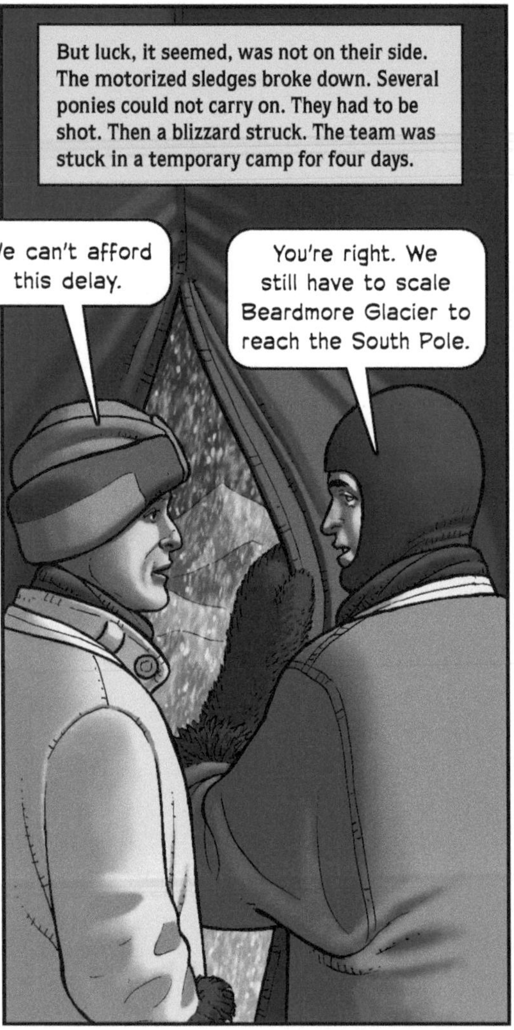
But luck, it seemed, was not on their side. The motorized sledges broke down. Several ponies could not carry on. They had to be shot. Then a blizzard struck. The team was stuck in a temporary camp for four days.
We can't afford this delay.
You're right. We still have to scale Beardmore Glacier to reach the South Pole.

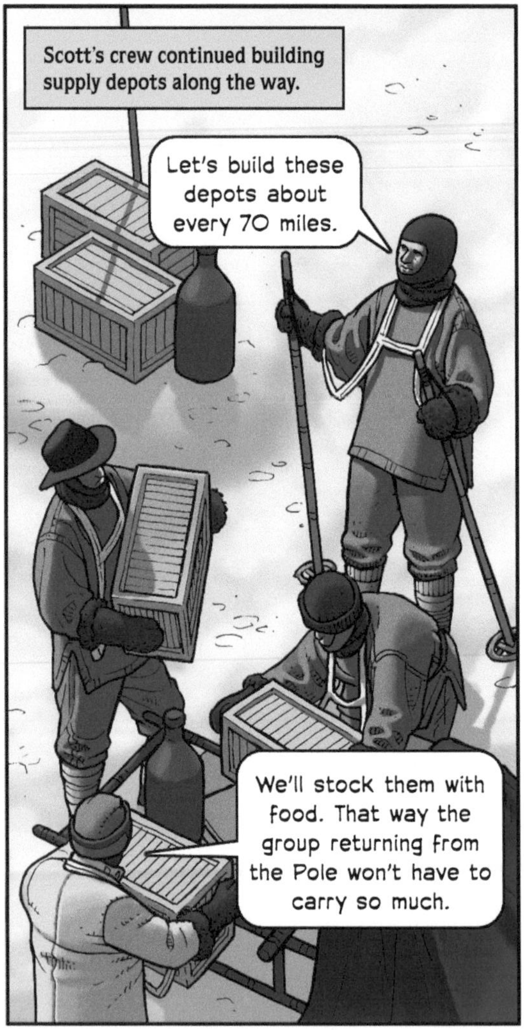
Scott's crew continued building supply depots along the way.
Let's build these depots about every 70 miles.
We'll stock them with food. That way the group returning from the Pole won't have to carry so much.

I'm sorry you must go back. We can't carry enough supplies for everyone to make the final journey to the Pole.

We must travel light to travel fast.

In December, Scott and his men reached Beardmore Glacier. They spent several weeks climbing it. Scott sent some men back to Cape Evans. They took the dogs with them. The ponies were shot and used for food.

What a way to celebrate your birthday!

On December 25, William Lashly fell into a deep crevasse. He dangled there for several tense minutes until the other team members pulled him up with a rope. It was his birthday.

I guess my present is that I'm still alive.

Later they had Christmas dinner in their tent. They ate pony meat, biscuits, pudding, and candy.

This is a real Christmas and birthday feast!

It almost makes me forget that we are thousands of miles from home.

In early January, the team reached the summit of Beardmore Glacier. Scott sent more men back to Cape Evans.

What a view!

It's all downhill from here. We should be just over 100 miles away from the Pole. If the weather is decent, we should average more than 10 miles each day.

At that rate, we will reach the Pole in less than two weeks.

Scott had planned to take Edgar Evans (not to be confused with second-in-command Edward Evans), Oates, and Wilson on the final journey with him to the Pole. At the last minute, he added Bowers to the list. These five men were called the Pole Party.

Little Bowers remains a marvel . . . no work is too hard.

Adding a fifth member to the party created challenges. The men shared food rations meant for four people.

We've got to make this food last, men.

They squeezed into a tent designed for four.

16

There were only four pairs of skis. The men on skis pulled the sledge. The fifth man trudged through the snow and ice on foot.

The five men kept pushing forward, eager to reach the Pole. Progress was slow, but spirits remained high. Scott was impressed with the men he chose for the task.

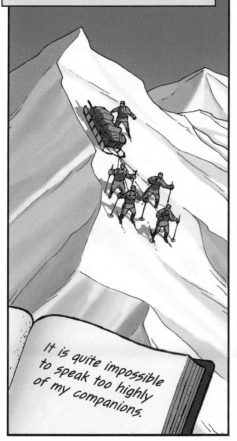

It is quite impossible to speak too highly of my companions.

The team tried to cover 10 miles (16 km) a day. On January 11, Scott thought they were about 74 miles (119 km) from the Pole.

Can we keep this up for seven days? None of us ever had such hard work before.

On January 15, Scott thought they could reach the Pole in two more days.

We are almost there. But have we beat Amundsen?

The next day, Scott's team spotted signs of a camp ahead of them.

They beat us! What a disappointment.

The Norwegians have been here!

Still, we must continue on to the Pole. We have come too far to stop now.

On January 17, Scott's team reached the South Pole.

We succeeded in reaching our goal. I just wish we could have been first.

We came all this way for nothing.

It's not a wasted trip. We still have all the scientific information we have gathered. But it IS disappointing to finish second.

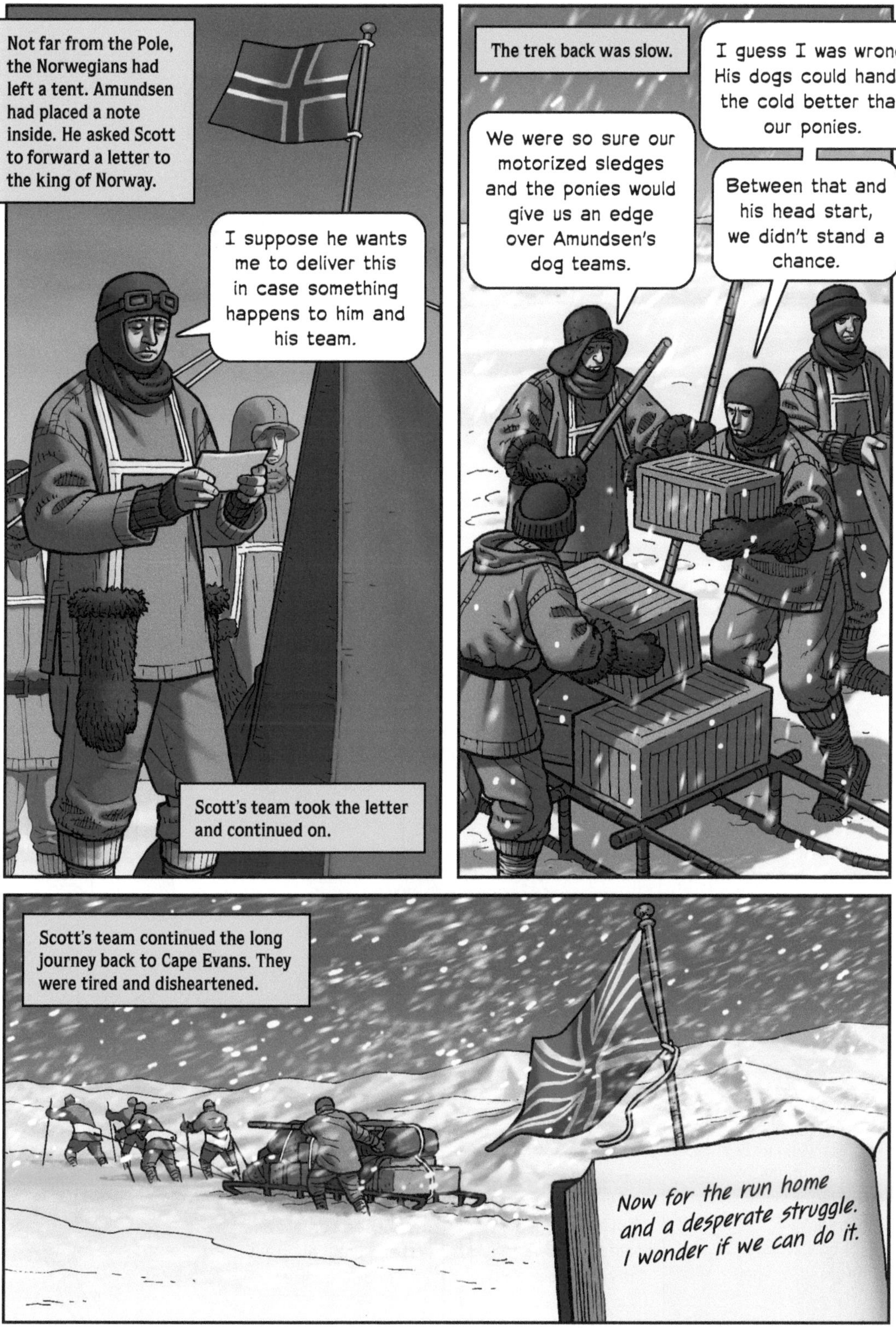
Not far from the Pole, the Norwegians had left a tent. Amundsen had placed a note inside. He asked Scott to forward a letter to the king of Norway.
I suppose he wants me to deliver this in case something happens to him and his team.
Scott's team took the letter and continued on.
The trek back was slow.
We were so sure our motorized sledges and the ponies would give us an edge over Amundsen's dog teams.
I guess I was wrong. His dogs could handle the cold better than our ponies.
Between that and his head start, we didn't stand a chance.
Scott's team continued the long journey back to Cape Evans. They were tired and disheartened.
Now for the run home and a desperate struggle. I wonder if we can do it.

Deadly Return

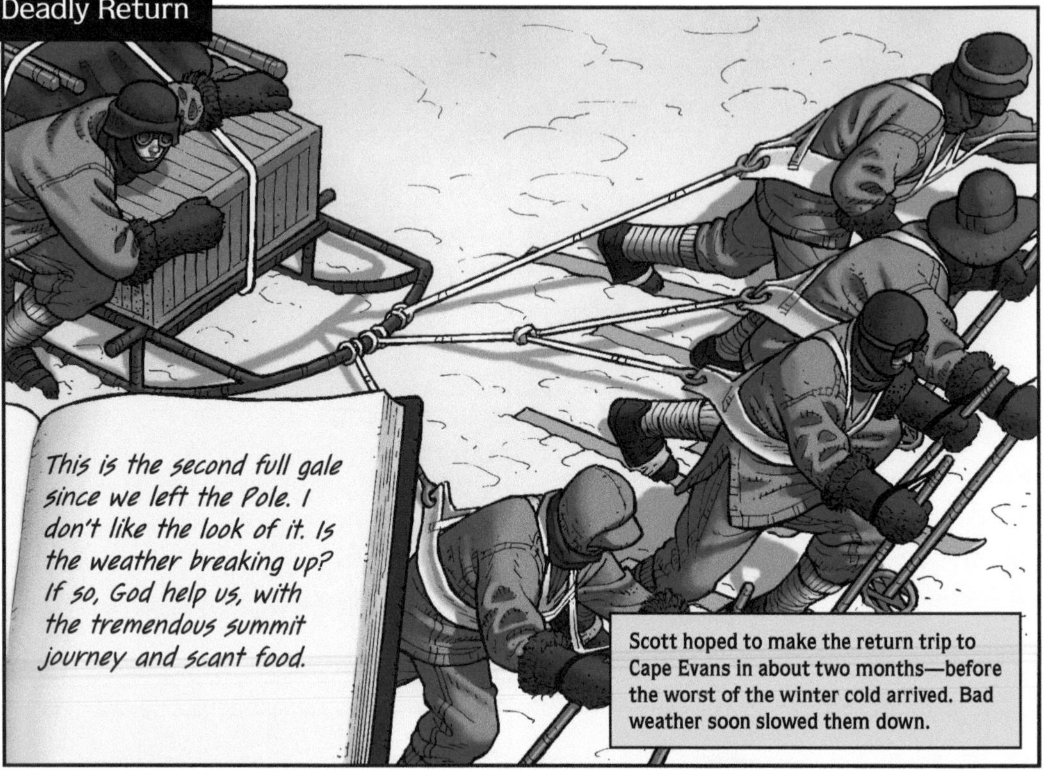
This is the second full gale since we left the Pole. I don't like the look of it. Is the weather breaking up? If so, God help us, with the tremendous summit journey and scant food.
Scott hoped to make the return trip to Cape Evans in about two months—before the worst of the winter cold arrived. Bad weather soon slowed them down.

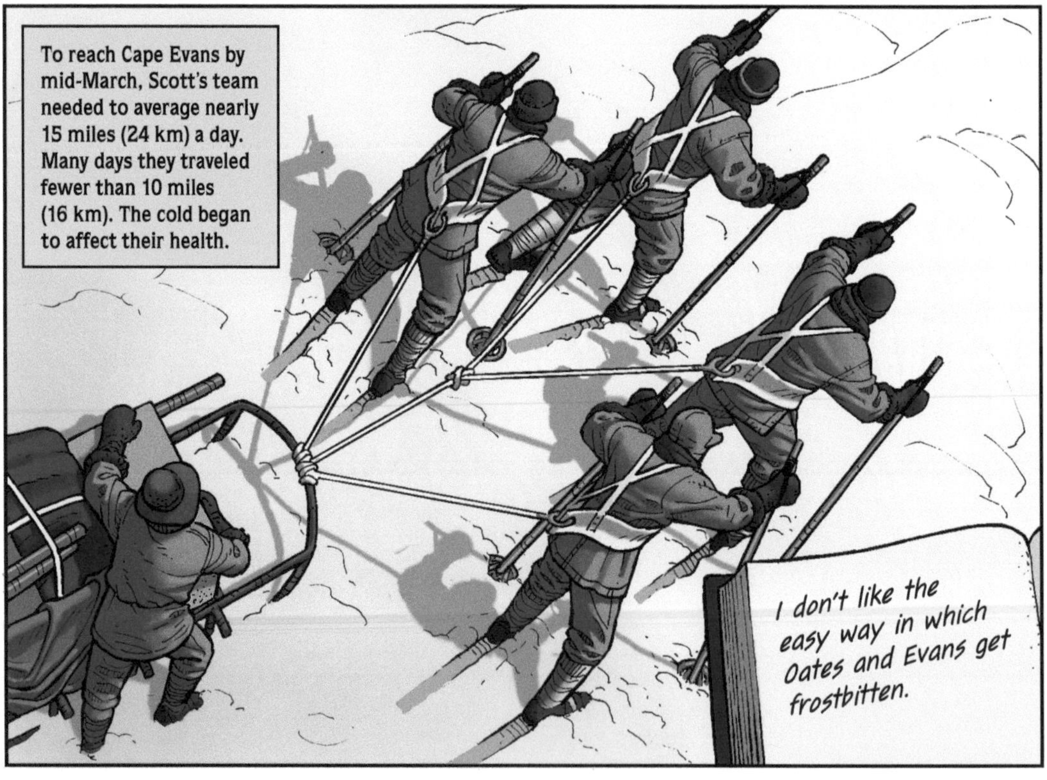
To reach Cape Evans by mid-March, Scott's team needed to average nearly 15 miles (24 km) a day. Many days they traveled fewer than 10 miles (16 km). The cold began to affect their health.
I don't like the easy way in which Oates and Evans get frostbitten.

On February 4, disaster nearly struck, as Scott and Evans fell into a crevasse. They somehow managed to climb back out.

Evans looks off. I wonder if he hit his head.

I thought that might be the end for us!

On February 12, the team drew near the next depot. Supplies were low. Could they reach it before their food ran out?

If we don't find that depot today, we may starve.

We'll find it. We have to. Evans is growing weaker. We all are. We need those supplies.

I'm really worried about Evans. He seems to be growing ever weaker.

I know. He is slowing down the pace. Still, we can't leave him behind.

Evans grew weaker. On February 17, he collapsed on the trail. He died that night.

Evans was a good man.

It is a terrible thing to lose a companion in this way.

But now we must push on and make sure WE survive.

On March 1, the temperature reached -40°F (-40°C). At that temperature, people can get frostbite even through layers of clothing. Oates had badly frostbitten feet.

This weather is colder than we predicted. How are your feet?

They feel numb. But I can keep going for now. I just hope the weather improves.

Let's hope winter hasn't arrived early.

About this time, a team from Cape Evans led by Cherry-Garrard reached the depot called One Ton Depot. They had come to resupply it for when Scott's team arrived.

Scott's team isn't expected here yet, are they?

No. Let's wait here a few days in case they arrive. They may need our help.

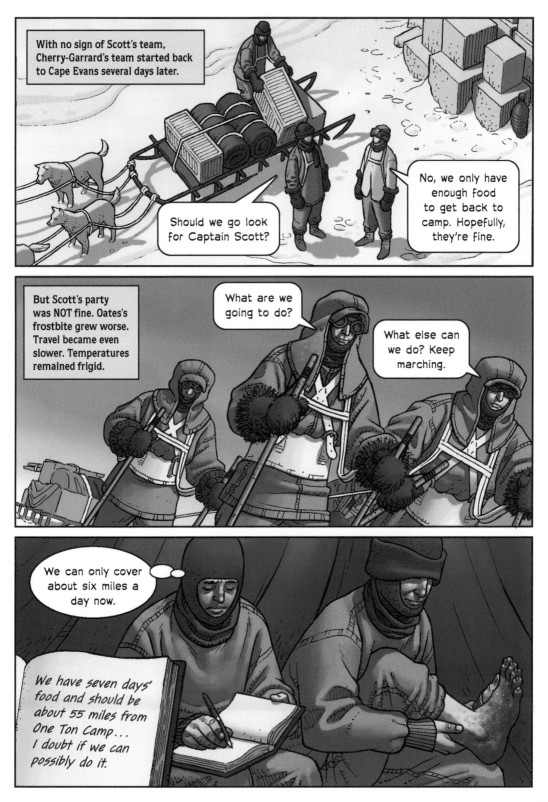

With no sign of Scott's team, Cherry-Garrard's team started back to Cape Evans several days later.

Should we go look for Captain Scott?

No, we only have enough food to get back to camp. Hopefully, they're fine.

But Scott's party was NOT fine. Oates's frostbite grew worse. Travel became even slower. Temperatures remained frigid.

What are we going to do?

What else can we do? Keep marching.

We can only cover about six miles a day now.

We have seven days' food and should be about 55 miles from One Ton Camp... I doubt if we can possibly do it.

By March 16, Oates could travel no further.

I am just going outside and may be some time.

Oates! No!

Please, don't!

Oates knew he was slowing down his team. By leaving, he hoped they would have a better chance to survive.

We knew that poor Oates was walking to his death, but though we tried to dissuade him, we knew it was the act of a brave man and an English gentleman.

Bowers, Wilson, and Scott plodded forward. By March 19, they were about 11 miles (18 km) from One Ton Depot.

All our feet are getting bad... Amputation is the least I can hope for now.

Then a blizzard struck. The weakened men could not even leave camp.

Blizzard bad as ever-Wilson and Bowers unable to start-tomorrow last chance-no fuel and only one or two (days) of food left-must be near the end.

The dying men wrote letters to their families. Scott wrote a message to the public.

We took risks, we knew we took them; things have come out against us . . .

On March 29, Scott made his final journal entry. He probably died soon after.

We shall stick it out to the end, but we are getting weaker of course, and the end cannot be far. It seems a pity but I do not think I can write more.

We have got to face it now. The Pole Party will not in all probability ever get back.

March dragged on with no sign of Scott's team. The men at the base camp grew worried. A group left on March 27 to search for Scott. Bad weather soon forced them back.

And we can't even go searching again for months. The weather is just too bad.

Finally, winter ended. In November, camp surgeon Edward L. Atkinson led a group looking for the lost explorers. On November 12, they spotted the tips of two skis poking above the snow.

They were so close to One Ton Depot. Had they reached it, they might have survived.

It's just terrible, Atkinson.

Scott, Bowers, and Wilson lay inside the tent. The Antarctic cold had kept the bodies intact.

It appears they died peacefully.

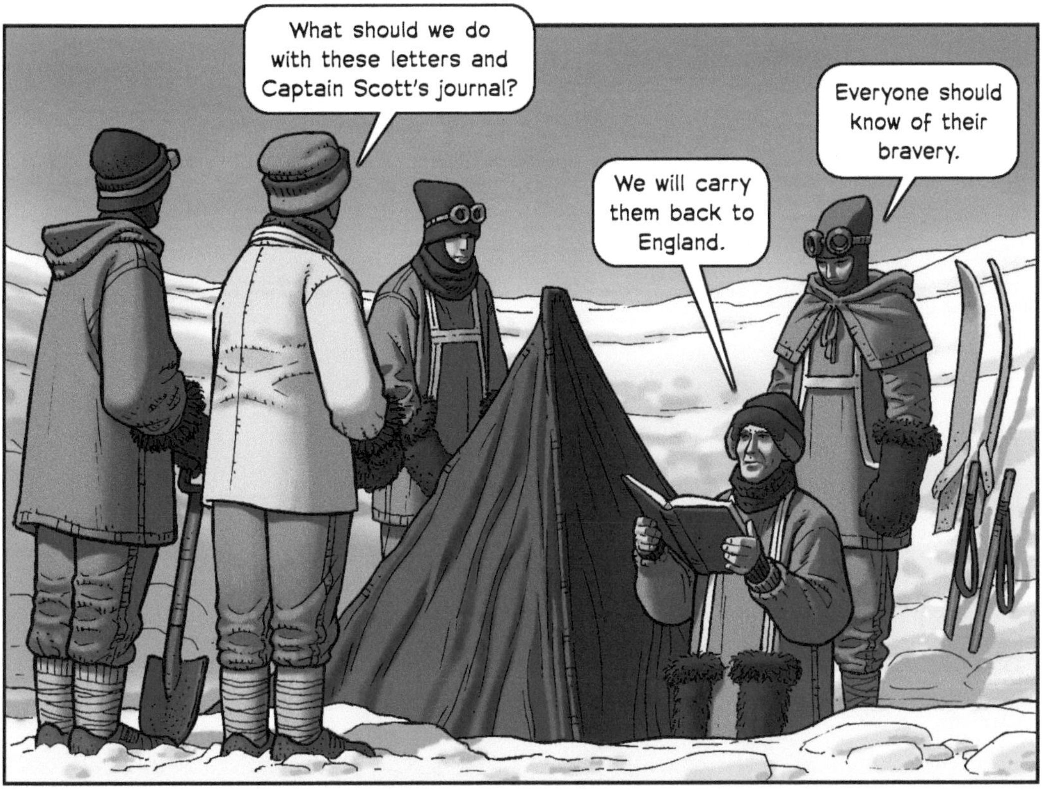
What should we do with these letters and Captain Scott's journal?
Everyone should know of their bravery.
We will carry them back to England.

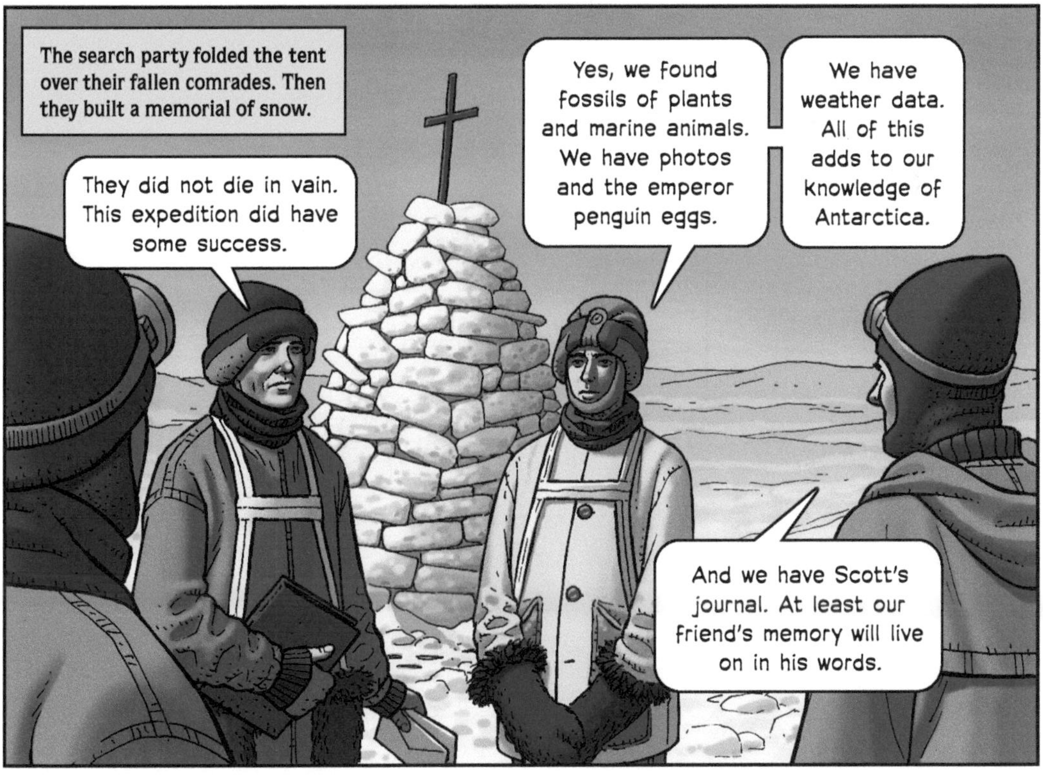
The search party folded the tent over their fallen comrades. Then they built a memorial of snow.
They did not die in vain. This expedition did have some success.
Yes, we found fossils of plants and marine animals. We have photos and the emperor penguin eggs.
We have weather data. All of this adds to our knowledge of Antarctica.
And we have Scott's journal. At least our friend's memory will live on in his words.

MAP OF THE EXPEDITION

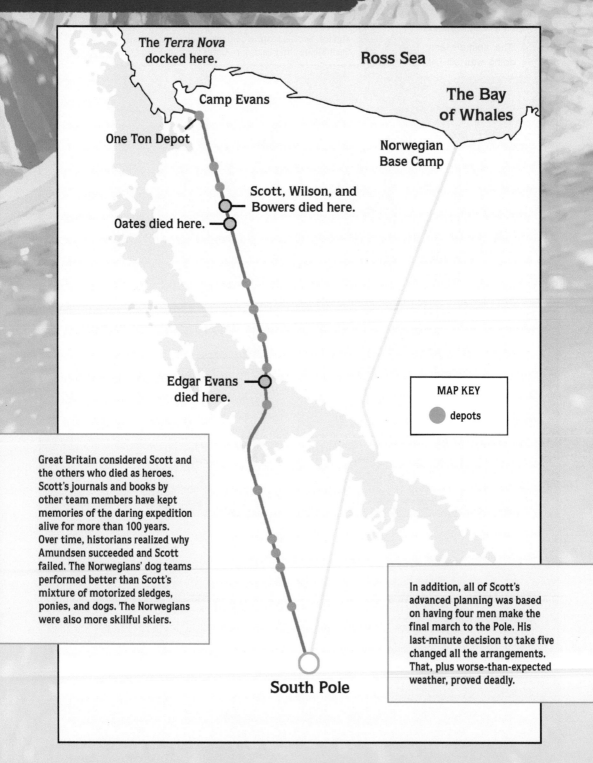

The *Terra Nova* docked here.

Ross Sea

Camp Evans

The Bay of Whales

One Ton Depot

Norwegian Base Camp

Scott, Wilson, and Bowers died here.

Oates died here.

Edgar Evans died here.

MAP KEY

● depots

Great Britain considered Scott and the others who died as heroes. Scott's journals and books by other team members have kept memories of the daring expedition alive for more than 100 years. Over time, historians realized why Amundsen succeeded and Scott failed. The Norwegians' dog teams performed better than Scott's mixture of motorized sledges, ponies, and dogs. The Norwegians were also more skillful skiers.

In addition, all of Scott's advanced planning was based on having four men make the final march to the Pole. His last-minute decision to take five changed all the arrangements. That, plus worse-than-expected weather, proved deadly.

South Pole

MORE ABOUT THE EXPEDITION

The hut at Cape Evans remains standing today. The cold weather has preserved everything. Items inside look almost the same as they did more than 100 years ago.

The distance from Scott's base camp to the South Pole and back was 1,766 miles (2,842 km). That's about as far as going from New York City to Wyoming.

The weather that Captain Scott's team faced was severe, even for Antarctica. For the last three weeks of their lives, they faced temperatures far colder than average for March. This, along with the blizzard that kept them from making a final push toward the next supply depot, doomed them.

Roald Amundsen's team of five men and 52 dogs left its base camp on October 19. They arrived at the South Pole on December 14. They left just two weeks before Scott's team, but they arrived at the Pole nearly five weeks earlier than Scott. Amundsen's team had good weather on the return trip. They reached their base camp in just over five weeks. Scott's return trip took more than two months. It ended in disaster.

One of the emperor penguin eggs from Scott's expedition is now on display at the Natural History Museum in London, England.

GLOSSARY

amputation (am-pyuh-TAY-shun)—the removal of a body part, such as a finger, toe, arm, or leg

crevasse (kri-VAS)—a deep, wide crack in a glacier or an ice sheet

depot (DEE-poh)—a place to store equipment or supplies

dissuade (dih-SWAYD)—to talk someone out of doing something

embryo (EM-bree-oh)—an animal organism in its early stages of development

expedition (ek-spuh-DI-shuhn)—a journey with a goal, such as exploring or searching for something

explorer (ik-SPLOR-uhr)—a person who travels into areas where no one else has been

frostbite (FRAWST-byt)—the freezing of skin or deeper layer of tissues on some part of the body

geography (jee-OG-ruh-fee)—the study of the earth's physical features

sledge (SLEJ)—a sled-like vehicle for hauling people or supplies over snow or ice

summit (SUHM-it)—the highest point of a mountain

READ MORE

Barone, Rebecca E. F. *Race to the Bottom of the Earth: Surviving Antarctica*. New York: Henry Holt and Company, 2021.

Fabiny, Sarah. *Where Is Antarctica?* New York: Penguin Workshop, an imprint of Penguin Random House, 2019.

Morlock, Rachael. *Roald Amundsen Reaches the South Pole*. New York: PowerKids Press, 2019.

INTERNET SITES

Antarctica Facts
kids-world-travel-guide.com/antarctica-facts.html

Antarctica—National Geographic Kids
kids.nationalgeographic.com/search?q=Antarctica&location=srp&type=manual

Britannica Kids—Robert Falcon Scott
kids.britannica.com/kids/article/Scott-Robert-Falcon/476314

INDEX

AUTHOR BIO

John Micklos, Jr. has written more than 50 children's books spanning a wide range of ages and genres. His work includes picture books, poetry books, and numerous nonfiction books. Popular titles include *One Leaf, Two Leaves, Count with Me!* (Penguin/ Nancy Paulsen Books, 2017) and *Raindrops to Rainbow* (Penguin Workshop, 2021).

ILLUSTRATOR BIO

Paul McCaffrey has worked is a freelance illustrator, mainly in the area of children's education. His clients have included NME, Vox, Punch, Deadline, Empire, CUP, OUP, Attack! Books, Macmillan, Harcourt, and Heinemann, amongst others. More recently, he has drawn comics for Marvel, DC, IDW, Thinkable, and Network Distribution. For Titan Comics, he has produced a number of covers as well as drawing *Anno Dracula 1895: Seven Days in Mayhem* and co-creating *Adler* with Lavie Tidhar. He lives in the UK with his wife and cat and far too many books than is good for him.